WHAT BOOKS PRESS

AN IMPRINT OF

THE GLASS TABLE

COLLECTIVE

LOS ANGELES

ALSO BY CATHY COLMAN

Borrowed Dress
Beauty's Tattoo

TIME
CRUNCH

CATHY COLMAN

WHAT
BOOKS
PRESS

LOS ANGELES

Publisher's Cataloging-In-Publication Data

Names: Colman, Cathy A., author.

Title: Time crunch / Cathy Colman.

Description: Los Angeles : What Books Press, [2019]

Identifiers: ISBN 9781532341465

Subjects: LCSH: Family--Poetry. | Physics--Poetry. | Art--Poetry. | Loss (Psychology)--Poetry. | Earth (Planet)--Poetry. | LCGFT: Poetry.

Classification: LCC PS3603.O463 T56 2019 | DDC 811/.6--dc23

Cover art: Gronk, *untitled*, watercolor and ink, 2018
Book design by Ash Good, www.ashgood.design

What Books Press
363 South Topanga Canyon Boulevard
Topanga, CA 90290

WHATBOOKSPRESS.COM

TIME
CRUNCH

For my dearest Aunt, Greta Ackerman—I'll miss you forever.

And for Richard Glatzer, darling friend, gone too soon.

The night knows nothing of the chants of night.
It is what it is as I am what I am:

—Wallace Stevens
from *Re-Statement of Romance*

CONTENTS

I

PHANTOM WEIGHT OF INFINITY

THE LAST TIME I SAW PAUL CÉZANNE

I could begin my life here. Wake up
to oranges and apples forever caught
in the bowl on the tablecloth with its frozen
leaves. Parallel melodies. Aubergines,
bloodrust and the secrets of grey—
earth's molten river-core

where colors erupt. Imagine
blue rushing back
from the country of its birth.
Nerve-like branches, dimmed
purple masses,
then yellow lightning, burnt
umbers soft
as distant thunder.
Every inch in present tense.

What is far away becomes
known as if the speed of my future
stopped here, where I no longer
have to be anything.
Not connect but dissolve. How
at the end everything was transparent—
vermillion, orpiment. Eternity
flashing and breaking

in the autumn of L'Estaque.
Half the landscape standing
in for the whole.
All my great loves lost but this.

HALF THE LANDSCAPE,

stands in for the whole, while I sit flaming
in my sheets, nerves hot as the pistil
of a burning lily. Did you know
that light instructs, illuminates,
but can't see itself? That light *itself* is blind?
You always knew I'd have to be a woman
who tries to break the code of heaven's
enigmatic billboard, to reconstruct each day out of
                    the stolen grammar of candles.

When I eat certain pharmaceuticals my body
spells itself like a telegram from the Buddha,
and sometimes I hear applause. Sometimes
I can still see the oxygen/hyacinth/speechless/
                    Cadillac radiance of everlasting earth.

"Each atom goes through all possible histories."
I found that on the ground on the back of a child's pink
index card defining "half-life": the time it takes for atoms'
disintegration in a radioactive substance. I'll tell you
what I've inherited: years that go in both
                    directions. No salt divinity here, no rain.

All night I dream of a new body.
                    Not next to me, but my own.

SELFISH, SELFISH JEWESS

Because I am the obvious choice for a sentry in this hidden army,
    for who knows what enemy
    from what century will try to breach my unsleep.
Because my bed is the country of my exile from the land of Morpheus
    and my sheets, a refugee's discarded clothes wet from drowning
    in the axed-over limbo waters.
Because the Earth has eleven magnetic poles and the ice-
    melt will cause the sea to drown me like a girl-child born in China.
Because I saw the dawn come up over the downs for the last time: absinthe
    and red poppies.
Because in the gunshot night I wore my dead father's iron voice as armor.
Because I couldn't understand why the night would never end
    and that the lantern sun would always unravel my nightgown
    into hieroglyphs. It took me days to translate all the words.
Because the Egyptians tattooed me and kept me in chains,
    my wrists only speaking when spoken to.
Because I didn't fear the dismantling—let it come with kerosene
    and a shovel, let it stagger
    up the basement stairs with its dry ice eyes.
What I feared was the *never-having-been*.
When was the last time I walked through clean snow with its
    precision kaleidoscope tatting?
Because the river is on fire and the water is on fire,
    running from faucets, ignition everywhere
like hundreds of cut-paper pieces blown from
    a windstorm into their own forest pyre.

Because I had trouble getting out of the car and the impatient
      man behind me rolled down his window and hissed,
      "You SELFish, SELFish Jewess!"
Because grief and morning are a passage into the unlived
      life where my old uniform, splayed in desert sand, exactly
      resembles a soldier's corpse.
Because my great-great-grandfather left Jerusalem at age 14
      and learned the tangled labyrinths of five languages before
      finally reaching Canada alone to start another tribe.
Because the white Russians starved us in the Pale, worked us until
      skin blew from our bones like winding sheets.
      And . . . we know what the Germans did.
Because I had a mania for scouring shadows on the floors, shadows
      that looked like blood let loose at the divination hour.
Because the wall behind my bed leads to Ben Shahn's red stairway
      which I climb with my one leg over this city's rubble, all under
      a thumbprint moon while my dead mother's voice sighs in my throat:
      My darling daughter, how much longer until I will see you again?
Because I have been so many women, none of them able to sleep.

BICKERING IN THE BATHROOM MIRROR

If only I could have rested
in a world of   knowable equations
before I was wedded upstream
in a churn of warning.
Our belongings,   the anchors
that sunk us deeper: your already crippled
raincoat falling   from the banister, Zig-Zag papers
on the spool table, batteries waiting in their
liminal lives for years, and throngs of T-shirts
and sweats   gnarled together   in the hamper
as if a killer instinct   had suddenly   gotten loose.
When we were still   at the threshold, particles
must have lost their hold on each   other, blown
into the   confetti of   petals, spindles from branches
unhinged from their limbs rained down
on us, a finely-honed chaos.   And by the end
of that long night, I was married   to someone
enthralled by the cadence   of an imaginary burglar's
footsteps,   oh, love   pacing the halls in the small
hours, bickering   with himself in the bathroom
mirror, drying his socks   over the stove
burners while he sat, studying   naked and beautiful in the kitchen
like a marble statue   of Anteros, learning yet
another doomed language.

VULTURES, WHEN THEY EAT
THEY'RE CALLED A WAKE

Two days one night with you painting the ceiling green
and making all the furniture face north so you have to stand up
to sit down because less meat is more meat, though you'll be
hungry for the rest of your life, because the future was so long ago
I can't remember it, and obstacles come from space and lay
down their heads in the grass. Even with wormholes
and budgets we can't get through to each other like when
we stayed up all night, stoned, laughing at music, and made
love in a Mendocino field before tourists ruined
everything, which is why you threw your glasses over the cliff
and yelled curses in Hungarian at a pine tree. And now we can't
navigate the badlands because I grew up with Clorox and
symbiosis and your parents were two ice cubes in a two-cube
tray. I now hear hammering outside that echoes forward into
the next year and makes history clear its throat to make room
for it on the platform. I mean, shelter is so fragile, eating and
sleeping moribund in the same bed and refugees fleeing in
grammarless boats where they can be hurt without words,
without contact sports, without yoga sprains. Take my knitted
vocabulary and make a scarf I can read to my tribe. It will be full
of lacunae which happens when no one speaks your language
because it's dying out. Take my dirt and I'll take
yours and maybe the earth will fecund again. I'm willing to lie
down if you are.

YOU, BACK FROM EXILE

Take a word, crosshair it into place
and let it begin its trajectory toward *l'ancien*.
Greek, Latin, hieroglyphics.

Whatness is concerned with content.
So many private horrors stink of kerosene, bloodsport.
Whereness is concerned with linkages.
We begin almost demented by the Big Bang accuracy
of metaphor. And the Word was...
Yes, we trusted the usher.

But the map—the points and symbols,
longing and attitude—
fails to deliver. It
caroms blindly into a mountain, like the blonde
movie star in her plane.

We are the ones who put life into stones and pebbles.
We had to invent art to understand nature.
She had to invent a self,
not to be crushed to death by it.

INCOMPLETENESS THEORY

But I want to tell you about

that evening I was locked in   the museum and
       smuggled food from the paintings:
Cézanne's rotten pears.
Magritte's huge apple.
Rembrandt's overcooked potatoes.

I want you to know

how I almost fell in love with
Degas' self-portrait.   His eyes empty
of dancers but full   of a fig's sweetness.

I came to see your kind of place.
We slow-danced naked,   as in
a low-budget film, out-of-sync looping,

blurred and blinded by too many lens flares, my ravenous
silverfish lingerie, peppered with holes.

I want to tell you

about the theory of incompleteness,
that in any   mathematical system
                there is always a question in
the language of that system that cannot be answered.

Now, as I lie
on the ink-spattered linoleum
that limns a map of the earth, my limbs
search for

the center of exactly what will hurt
the most.
Inside the aphotic zone, becalmed,
    I feel my finger on   the horse latitudes
where sailors had to heave

the great beautiful   beasts overboard to save
on weight and water.

    I want you to know

You touched my riverbed hair
in lost, wrung-out dawn   and now I'm falling
through winter's painted carapace, and
I see myself,   I want myself,   without you
                        everywhere, starving.

LEDA, OUTSIDE BISBEE, ARIZONA

. . . . another unslept night   outside, the catclaw

trees, knife-grass

drawn from *Dr. Caligari's Cabinet.*

    I'm bleached by moonlight.

I cover myself with the autobiography of

a frayed blanket, dissonant wind

chimes,

mother's far away sea-voice.

Nothing works so I go back   to the bar

where he still sits clutching

gold rush brew   nothing between us

except his salt

breath   a large man, like a chunk of broken off

    mountain.

. . . and suddenly we're

in the weeds   he wants me to be nothing, *his*

nothing, just like my father did.

    He wants me like that,   prime-

numbered and factored-out, wearing infinity's

clothes.   He enters me rutting, his weight pinning me

as if gravity gave him an extra dose.

I dig my nails into the hard winter

of his back, bite   his leathery shoulder

. . . . then he's gone as I lie under the neon

    sign: *Vacancy*

I strip off to

burrow into my

        bed,   the stirred-up

dark   like river dirt

in a storm   rolling over and over,

        writhing with nearly visible

snakes   when daybreak forces

itself into my eyes

    and I pull another

feather   from my mouth . . .

THE LAST TIME I SAW SAMUEL BECKETT

Instead of a partial object, a total object with missing parts

as in the universe

that is 80% dark matter, which we know

exists only

because of its pull on what we *can* see, planets and tides

and galaxy clusters

moving much faster than their weight allows, strange,

circumnavigating

their own clichés. Dark matter that is dark yet also transparent

as if

when I am heard, I can no longer be seen.

Or if

seen, being born but not asking

to be.

Father tamping down light until it learns to tamp itself.

Until just

a painted mouth, the brevity of red talking in its slumber,

as if

a whole other existence waits for me

at the gate

of a factory that manufactures ether. Or outside

a silent but crowded

ballroom. While the two men talk and disregard me:

the ragged tree—

Nothing is funnier than unhappiness.

All objects fall in the same way. If you happen

to look up.

II

TOSSING FROM TURNING

TIME CRUNCH

Seems like either Virginia Woolf,
Gerard Manley Hopkins or Theodore Roethke made
            me pregnant. It started when I decided to build

a chart of the universe to connect them for my
Master's degree. Maybe all that in-seeing + greenhouse fertilizer
            +Vita Sackville-West's love letters . . .

I suddenly found the cow-dung smell of coffee and musky children
impossible then. I wanted it out of me:
            nose-nub, grey fortune cookie,—out,

what some call slaughter
of the innocents, just let the *manshape, that shone sheer*
            off, disseveral, cut away the roots,

which were connected to the sounds of words, but
it was sharper than that, the salty, slightly rotting ocean-tang
            which can mean new life.

Eyes closed, I imagined a clean, white
room, box of bees' wax-light
            candle inventing a glow-color,

half cream, half queen. She's willing
to lend me her stillness, but time, *this urge, wrestle, this*
            resurrection of dried sticks, is not. Time,

scientists think now, is rushing toward The Big Crunch.
How at a certain point, gravity will reverse
            time's arrow and the expanding

universe will snap back like a rubber band and become pregnant
with itself, *with the world entire maybe,*
            I am outside of it crying 'Oh save me from

being blown forever outside the loop of time, Or maybe I'd see my long-
term lovers: one with a flute and scars from burning leaves; another
            with jazz and continuous self-soothing rocking.

I'd see my mother in her absolute-blue house dress, fresh from
digging radishes, my brother and me eating Fig Newtons
            watching *The Early Show* —maybe this

reversal might be just the thing
to let me skip over this trance of machines and breathe
            underwater, a gilly-girl again,

while the dawn factories gut the world with weapons
and children are glutted with Celan's *black*
            milk of daybreak,

hungry, hungry for my grandmother's chicken
liver, and maybe I won't have to
              see all the things I can't bear

to see: the heads will stitch themselves
back onto bodies, and the crosses will burn—
              like Tiki torches—themselves out.

BODY POLITICS

"Perspective is as accidental a thing as lightning."
—Jacques Rivière, 1912

And if you think about it, the word free conjures voting and
animals leaping back to the wild and here, I put my head on
your shoulder in the 1950s, even before I was born, and
it's still there watching *Rebel Without A Cause* but we have a cause
to be hyper-aware, so if you're reading this, it's too late because
the fair is closed and the unfair is open, the whole country alight
with uncivil rites, and if you think about it the word free also
conjures fighters and couches on the curb and everyone doing
a shaky dance with congas and even snakes fleeing from their
charmers and if he says he's a woman, he's a woman and I'm
a man, and if I say I'm a man, then he's still a woman, so bake
the wedding cake with a lucky coin inside, drown the hall
in purple hydrangeas until we eat, drink, and bypass the sale
that says *Everything Must Go* because scientists have taken
the first ever photograph of light as both a wave and a particle
which explains so much about swimming and kissing and that old
electricity that ignited between us when you passed the beer and
our fingers got entangled forever, and all I can do is go to sleep
to trucks striking their tires on the curb which sounds like
the percussion in Stravinsky's *Rite of Spring*, and dream of the dot
and the line, a kind of Morse Code that says, I'm still alive,
what about you?

THE LAST TIME I SAW VIRGINIA WOOLF

My friend who's bipolar told me she checks
herself into the psychiatric ward once a month
for a tune up. When they ask her if she's homicidal
or suicidal she always answers, "Both."
Having the correct name for something doesn't cure it.
PMS. PTSD. MIA. DOA.
Acronyms try too hard to make friends.
They say the Himalayas of my brainwaves point to trauma.
I still get postcards from my childhood that say
"Wish you weren't here."
P.S. I've had my fill of paeans to Pfizer.
There's a fascist inside me who is always smoking on the veranda
waiting for his name to come up on my dance-card.
I hear the militias forming in the back woods.
I hate these men with guns.
But to be honest, haven't I, all this time,
just been waiting
for the right river, the right weapon?

DEAR WATER

But, listen, you need to know: death

is nothing. It makes no sound or it becomes a sudden

clearing on the parched earth

with one low-pitched haunting of a cello.

Music's primary illusion is passing time.

This is only part of the story.

Science says that everything is Maya: a pock-marked

sea face, white sky around twisted lilac,

walnut cracked open to reveal its sweet, witless brain.

The sky is now an interrogatory blue

like mother's opal, her music of St. Petersburg

marking another drought year. In the constellation

Cassiopeia, she suffers upside-down, chained

to her chair, a silver noise in the luster of the dented cup

hit against it, in the longing for milk.

Sometimes you feel part monster, part witness to the climb

   of global heat, its fake absence of evidence.

Whenever I enter a room,

I discover the body has amnesia: it has forgotten where

the aviary of music goes, the wet smell

   of eucalyptus.

Outside, the sprinklers conjure mirages

from the sidewalk. They shimmer like miracles everyone's

used to. Water wheel and the song behind

   all this, white noise thrashing

in the river's sprawled braille of

pebbles washing downstream with overtones only

musicians can hear, as the Milky Way sings

    its motherly opera overhead.

Weather builds in the conservatory,

    Castor and Pollux cast their net on the sea,

while billions of dust atoms rain through us

from the jigsaw puzzle of galaxies. And there's that

iridescent green beetle I've tracked

    through ruins of onion grass, past

signs saying how high the tsunami will be during an earthquake,

past my body and its glittering

    thirst, past a wilderness

of sweat wanting rain in a habitat

of scrublands with cacti blooming meaty flowers, biospheres with orange

Humboldt lilies, speckled,

                       open wide in lust's unreason.

      Dear Water,

we are entwined the way I am with music,

 perfectly and inexactly. In the mud

foundry, away from famine, away

from this 3 A.M. body, the infinite labyrinths

                     of self-harm— Dear Water,

I want them to bury me

     inside you.

DREAM HOUSE

"Allow me to ignore that description of a room."
—André Breton

I go into the kitchen and lie down on the couch,
throw hard-boiled eggs into the fireplace.

What wall separates tossing from turning? Which room
knows enough Chinese to make the rug lie down?

This house has lost its memory. Every day when I wake
up, it has forgotten where the piano goes.

Just a minute ago, I was reading Bachelard
on the discontinuity of time. It made sense then. Now

I can't find scissors anywhere. I need them to cut my bangs
over the computer. I open the freezer and find the TV.

Of course, it's on CSPAN. I'm starting to get angry.
Someone said defrost anger and you get grief.

Or was that turkey and gravy? That person also folded
the blanket down on my bed in the garage.

Beech trees aren't supposed to grow in southern California.
Two of them intertwine like vertebrates as they stand

dying in my only bathroom. Their fatal leaves fall into the toilet.
The crawl space where the praying mantises live is sometimes

the attic. This house doesn't have an attic. So you can see
my confusion. This house has forgotten more than I can

remember, deep in the drawers, closets, dusty thin lips of
old file folders. A chair I've rarely paid attention to, finally

turns its back on me. The oven, ditto.

THE LAST TIME I SAW ANTONIN ARTAUD

I fell in love with your face or maybe not your face
but the lack of delirium in your eyes in the film *Napoleon*,
your jaw so beautiful it should have been breaking news or maybe
not news but something setting off bells, an alarm that portended

the pitch of your lecture on the Plague which was not a lecture
but an enactment of someone coming down with the Plague,
who made the theatre not only find its double
but its cannibal or maybe not its cannibal but its

voraciousness like an undercurrent that pulled
down Icarus and his burnt wings.
You, who as a teenager were stabbed in the back by a pimp in Paris
for no reason, whose somnambulism woke other sleepers fumbling

in their beds or maybe not their beds but their army cots and then
the sanitarium where you remembered you owned the twisted
walking stick that belonged not only to Jesus and Lucifer but to
St. Patrick and you tried to return it to Ireland where

you were put in a straitjacket. Or maybe not a straitjacket but
a closer-fitting suit, a bespoke suit, or maybe a costume
you'd wear for the rest of your life, while you dragged the sun
and litmus paper moon on stage, both visible in the same hour or

maybe not an hour but an intermittent infinity, found in the soft spot
of your madness, your godless mouth full with scatological oaths
and screams, the hissing of snakes and glossolalia after the camera
flickered over your skin shimmering as you played Marat

or maybe not your skin but a fiery field from which you can't
escape or maybe not escape but enter the room
where you died, sitting at the foot of the bed,
holding your shoe.

III

I BELIEVED I WAS LEVITATING

THE LAST TIME I SAW KURT SCHWITTERS

Und Merz

instead, we talked of dogs,

we corresponded yet we were still

    in the age of slaughter

    with the Dada distance of history, here and there

a Jew, bread

peeking from the dead man's jacket pocket, more mud than

bread. Everything had broken down,

    a woman who had integrated

a pair of binoculars

a pair of large, black mammals

feline panthers,

the tail, the hind legs, the glistening coat

    a gaggle of people

it was like a revolution

I believed I was levitating

height, weight, sex, speed, mood

not as it was— behind us,

      parched fields and marshland,

the whole clearing gone very bright within me

      a Prussian blue

spears of smoldering crimson

a plateau of dazzling

woodcocks from Siberia or Chernobyl loaded

with brass bullets

      —but as it should have been . . .

for starters, it was an accident.

DIORAMA

There is a problem in all this.

The fact that, if nothing else,
as Proust says,
we still have our childhoods to write about—
but many words and passages have been redacted
or quick-frozen from mine.
  My obsession with homunculi.

I owned a fully adult woman and man.
They taught me about frisson and sex. About
enjoying the power I had over them
because they were small
and I could make them do anything.
  Of course, I did.

When I was 12, someone set our house on fire.
The two Ford Valiants, trapped in the garage, brave ones,
burned to skeletons as did family pictures, you know, the ones that
look like you but are actually pictures of time. The ashes flew up like
feathers, bad weather over the house,
saved because someone pounded on our front door at 3 AM, screaming,
  "Get out! Get out!"

All our Jewish and non-Jewish neighbors stood
around the fire, everyone weeping in their night
clothes like a zombie funeral.
And my dad was crying, and Alice next door said, "You didn't need

those cars anyway, Henry, did you now?" The police
thought it might be a hate crime. Though "hate crime"
was not a phrase used then. They never did catch the arsonist.
Sometimes I think it was me.

        Because back in my room I saw the holy
aqua-glow aquarium with the miniature
Atlantis, a castle I believed I would discover
and live in some day. There was always
a little gloom painted into the corners
of our house so we didn't forget ourselves. And
we held a soupçon of belladonna on our
tongues when the lights went out
        and the moon was a disappearing communion wafer.

        Somewhere in that house there was
a golem, who opened eyes in the knotty pine.
Watching us sleep and eat Wonder Bread, mayonnaise,
bologna. We sang Christmas carols and hymns
        my mother played from songbooks with pages

fresh as sheets laundered on the line.
That hexagon merry-go-round with
wooden clothespins:
each blouse, each work shirt and pair of
striped pajamas pinned
between earth and sky,

      empty as light.

JEWISH PARTY

Each pill in its plastic jar, each scar
in its flesh-longitude, those old stills—
thick with spit-shined razor wire, with the dead
in piles like twisted reams of fabric—all
remind us of how good time can be:
It can stop.   We see
the photograph, only a moment, words
stoppered inside the bodies
that made them the bodies
inside the images—
invisible elision, silent, as they
cross from being to become.
Like children
among them.   Who saw the
piles of shoes, eyeglasses, skulls and bones
made into lovely chandeliers
and sconces? We, who have always hidden
ourselves in the tacit of now: we are
not them, never them.   We
wanted to live in the in-between
because we thought   we would not suffer
there. But suffering is free
to see anyone   it wants any time,
like imperfections in old wood on the ceiling
that make trapped, psychotic
faces—a whole party of them   clinking ice cubes

in tall bar glasses that I heard
from my bedroom when
my parents had guests in our tract home
where every house was laid out   the same
way so when you dreamt, you
dreamt of another house,
exactly   like yours
but with different   sometimes very few
signs of life.

WHILE DEUTERIUM AND TRITIUM SPREAD

through animal and mineral, braiding
through my hair,
throwing open the window to the sky's
cracked plate
of oysters and pearls, as

the clouds' gold isotopes sail
through middle air's
muddle, I can smell the wet pavement
from childhood rain
coming, drops large as a giant's
tears when my mother runs
from the house to get us out
of the plastic pool away from
lightning— I am struck.

I am struck like a rescue drum, by
my own heartbeat scaring
me up again from this near collision
of elements, the past
eating the present so it can steal
my purse's money, a bouquet
of paper orchids, from the future.

The window is open, part of the dangerous
hive mind right before
it rains, where my mother sits in death's plastic
pool, blue pearls falling
from her mouth, before I wake to braid
my own hair here, years ago where
the future waits off stage.

SHE RECOUNTS THE AMNESIA
OF THE FUTURE

Now you know better,
everything's worse than before and better,
even though you're no longer brave enough
to eat raw tuna, or swim to the pier at midnight,
drive the 110 so fast your neck's almost snapped off,
the ache of time pulling itself loose from the commitment
of space, the bloody frescoes and keening cathedrals
of the last fuck, the last war,

that sterile walk on the moon
while we danced the hullabaloo,
then sprinted from elevators with briefcases chained
to our wrists—*breathe, dammit, breathe*—
your body says, (a drunken specimen of repetition,
though no wine has passed your lips) when you can't sleep

a prayer that your mania for harm
will be snuffed out, though you feel naked in the sun *inside*
your house and your open-eyed insomniac asks for you:
do you read Fenallosa to discover
why the Chinese ideogram drove Pound so wild, why
he couldn't lie flat enough? Do you listen
to Thomas Bernhard's inspired whining or read
Darwin on his finches, finding the voice of a stranger
misdialed on the telephone more intimate than you expected?

No, you watch the Marx Brothers on roller skates
in *The Big Store,* bring anarchy into your bedroom
where it belongs, where you can stroke it, make it bigger,
which is why you no longer have a signature,
well, it's just a straight line, a way of turning
the other cheek to capitalism for you must offer
your landlord something: the pomegranate
cracked open with its cache of rubies is not enough.

You've abandoned your orchard and the ground runs
with the soft guts of crushed oranges and early plums.
Have you noticed how neatly water mends itself?
Maybe you are your own rescuer and you're calling
to yourself before you die of exposure. "Over here,"
across this bridge's sudden amnesia,
"I'm over here."

THE LAST TIME I SAW JANIS JOPLIN

Just say yes to drugs, *come on, take it* for pain,
    insomnia, heartbreak, take your pick,
with their I am sick-sick and so very well,
  too well, washed down with Jack, to molder or lodge in your liver.

  I'm X-ray vision. Songs about knives and a Mexican opal
on my finger. With buoyancy before drowning,
   the salvation-pulse-technology, that buzzbuzz
between utterances, console-me chaos, *make me feel good*, yes.

    Without them
  I'm a bad translation of the *Bhagavad Gita*,
     a quantum cup of joe that stings like speed
shot in your vein, a wound zipped shut so tight
     the bloodroot must suffer its unholy itch.

 If only I could disguise myself as summer: *never, never, never*—
   its hot, gleaming boulevards stretched out like musclemen.
Those rollercoaster sunsets with their pawnbroker silvers and golds,
     and half-naked, adolescent dawns.

 Just say yes, *take another little piece*, fondle
    the red oblong queen, hum the oval blues baby blues,
  the yellow I'm-so-lonesome-for-you,
   my quarry, my ghost-girl . . .

IV

AND EVERYWHERE PRECIPICE

THE LAST TIME I SAW DELPHINE SEYRIG

No one will give you a map. Little flutter-by,
     your elbow bent, hand resting
on your shoulder near the ropes of the neck,
     resting like a wing not beating.
Didn't I meet you last year in the garden
     where humans cast shadows
but objects don't?

You glide around the same corners as if
     the reappearance of a familiar
corridor newly traversed were a cliff.
     Didn't I meet you last year at the Gestalt convention
where we all stood in for each other? My breath

     trapped in its paper cage. You, at the Grand Ball,
wearing your Chanel hoard-of-blooms,
     white as a fossil. Your body more vassal than vessel.
Even as the barometer dropped and we rushed
     outside where the wind was just a start-up business,
and the sculptures were doomed to re-anoint themselves
     with last season's light, didn't I meet you on the balcony's

blank page, last year like now, no real past nor present,
     just an almost-between-us?

THE MOTHS

Moth-ers are people who hunt moths.

Flicking their paper wings, wings

    more hyaline than eyelids, than pages

in a miniature Tibetan Book of the Dead.

    They can never get close enough.

Driven mad by this false moon's proximity,

    they can't reach her heat.

Just as I, not anchored to anything,

can never, for even one blinding second, touch

    again, my mother, moth mother,

my Incandescent,—

    This is not hunger or thirst.

That lovely fix, She, the light, is their only way

    home from the closed specimen

box of darkness.

FROM AN IMPRINT

There's never enough sun in the tiny room
where my almost weightless father
has had gravity's forgetfulness fever the heft out of him.

Cobalt shadows on his face, fingernails like horn,
water glass through which patches like trod-on leaves
show crimson on his hands.

I am intoxicated by loss that courses on
in its entrepreneurial fervor: his skin loosening, his
left eye always closed.

When he looks at me suddenly, his right eye stops.
It has found something— it glitters hard,
unfamiliar like newly formed quartz cracked

green by day. The eye is discerning, angry
yet relieved that I am all it recognizes.

ECLIPSE

Every wrought scene holds

the phantom weight of infinity

when viewed through a pinhole

in cardboard,

through the telescope of years,

all that dark matter

like uncurtains snagging themselves

on the stars.

ON THE OCCASION OF THE NAUTILUS SHELL

And everything slovenly.

And everything rollicking.

And everywhere precipice.

And nothing calendar.

And everything Michelangelo.

And everything drive-in French movie.

And everywhere grey ear of morning.

And everywhere amplify.

And everything howl.

And blank day of her death.

And everything wield.

And everything calculate.

And everything glissando.

And nothing apparel.

And everything slowing down suddenly.

TWO MIRRORS FACING EACH OTHER

Sometimes I get infinity and eternity confused:
I looked at the sun, her face, too long, because
it was the last time.
She was dressed in her best outfit. The Armani
suit with the black shiny beads, the one
she had worn on her birthday last year.
Silence poured from her as if funneled
from a well at the center of the earth.
I asked the man in blue-striped
coveralls for scissors. Earlier, in a more officious
room, he had worn a suit and tie
when my brother and I had to pick out a coffin
from a thick, glossy catalogue. Pictures of coffins, each
in a plastic sleeve, escalating in price. What would Mom like?
We passed on the "Elvis" coffin, all silver-shot and
pearlescent, and went with traditional New England.
The man had given us their branded "Dignity"
water, green canvas "Dignity" tote bags, and vault brochures.
There's one open next to your mother's, he had said looking
pointedly at me.
Now in his work duds, he walked over noiselessly and
handed me the scissors. Perhaps I was in shock, but I never
saw him leave the room to get them. I took a "Dignity" tissue
from the pack. I cut a piece of her late autumn hair.
It smelled sickly sweet, like when I had
dissected a frog in physiology.

I wanted to kiss her
but I was too short to reach her in the coffin. He watched me
steadily from a distance as if he were guarding my mother's
corpse. Did he think I'd lift her and dance wildly
across the linoleum, her head on my shoulder?
When we did dance we were always in the kitchen with
the beige tile floor and Tommy Dorsey on high. She taught
me The Lindy and she would always lead. That shape
we made and the mixed clacking sounds of our feet, her
energy shivering like a divining rod when it finds
water as she guided me firmly into
the right steps, won't be listed in death's little black book, death's
polymath rhetoric. No. It will stay in me. Just as I will
always hear the complex yet bright lexicon
of her fingers on the piano keys; her bell-like
touch trilling through our house and
from the stage. What I wanted to say is "Don't touch
her. She's mine."
A few weeks ago, I took
the hair that I had tied
with black ribbon from its envelope.
It was soft and glossy as a baby's.
It smelled like nothing.

THE LAST TIME I HEARD THELONIUS SPHERE MONK

Water in the gutter sounds
    like bebop and the gravel like hard
bop   while I worry my
worry beads waiting for you   to come
    back, my echo-in-the-stairwell
man.   You're like

a record snowfall, once   you're here
    we can't get out   of the house. We
feed the cats cottage cheese
    and pretend   we're dieting in
the bomb shelter because the   cirrus

and cumulus from Washington, D. C., are lowering, dark-
    ening and   darkling, listen to the   news and
there may be a tinny voice that warns us bad
    acid   is being   sold on 7th Avenue and
sarin in Syria,   because we are
in the crosshairs of   I lied and

fucking   shut up, subliminal like   between
          seconds and sub-lingual   like your tongue
enmeshed with mine. I'm   waiting for our early
          amphibious natures to drag us back into
the feracious water   so we can

rebirth ourselves   not like   Christians
          but like fish with feet   who walk
on golf   courses   in Florida though   darling
          we'll probably end up voting Republican
because it's too bright   to see or read

a book where   a woman   waits   on a Greek
          island   for a poem to come   to her like
a trained dog but   without pipe bombs   and
          gun shells in the backyard,   relics   from our
on-going   civil   wars. Not just the countries' but

ours because we   tried couples   counseling and
          it always boils   down to either
a Segway or a boy's choir and sometimes
          a telegram that's taken   so long to reach
us   it just says   Stop. Stop. Stop.

EVERYTHING MUST GO

Beaumont, Texas, produces the saddest Tweets.

Ask a willow tree in Beaumont to do the weeping for you.
They would in Texas. They have their own
power grid. Home-grown militias with matching
beards and shotguns. Open carry. All the sex
on the outside. If you do it
with a body that looks like yours, they might
kill you. I look inside my body
for my girlfriend. She's gone
ten years now. Eye cancer.

CUT TO

the father straddles her
on her bedroom floor,
trying to saw off her hair with a butter knife.

Thomas Edison, inventor of the light bulb, was afraid of the dark.

As Jupiter rises into the inky sky, near the moon's
fingernail clipping, I feel I might break apart. I've
been so busy avoiding black ice and alleys I'd almost
forgotten the windowless room where you took something
from me. Was it my first design—the patent for the electrovote
recorder? You've brought on mudslide-in-the-laboratory,

winter's indigo paintbrush, sky and earth draped
in grey mourning. It wasn't my fault I had to stay
in that boxcar all night with every size needle, corks,
wires, screws, all types of hoofs and hair of goats, horses,
minx, camels. I needed them. I didn't mean to set the car on fire—
all I wanted was a candle!

FADE TO BLACK

WRITTEN IN WHITE ON A BLACK SCREEN

It seems that today one's poems aren't taken seriously unless
they have a reference to St. Augustine and his confessions.

FADE TO WHITE

The electric chair was invented by a dentist.

This feels like a natural leap.
As the dentist stares into my mouth, he also
sees the infinite.
When he drills, I am shocked into forgetting
everything but the vortex of pain. Almost like
birth. Novocain wears
off fast. He asks me to open my mouth
so wide I can hear black-sound water. I feel
like my skeleton might turn inside out
and end up dead in a dirty green motel room
with amateur portraits of Inuits on the walls.

CLOSE ON

a CSI team bagging blood samples from
the sheets: a pink clutch and one pink, low-heeled pump.

My murderer turns out
to be my boyfriend, even
though from his profile
I thought he wasn't the jealous type.
He asks for steak, corn on the cob,
and chocolate cake with walnuts
for his last meal.
He will not get to floss.
Normally, I would not joke about the death penalty
because I believe it is barbaric and should be outlawed
in every state.

Every year, over 2500 left-handed people are killed by using products
made for right-handed people.

INT. LIVING ROOM – DAY

I am a left-handed person and I almost killed my father
when I was seven while using a right-handed scissors
to shirr a ribbon.
He sits next to me on the plaid couch and the blade
hits an artery in his arm.

MATCH CUT TO:

Water spouts
from the Whites Only drinking fountain.
Blood spatter leaves pictographs on the white shag carpet.
The sky looks singed and empty.
The love I have for my father curls and starves into itself,
then tries to come closer like a punished dog.
I run and hide under the bed.

One in every 4 Americans has appeared on television!

FLASHBACK:

I am five, wearing a white crinoline, sitting in the bleachers
in the Peanut Gallery on the *Howdy Doody Show*. My father
is somewhere in the deep sound stage.
Buffalo Bob's faceted jeweled belt glows
like the Aurora Borealis.
I have a crush on the show's Native American puppet,
Princess Summerfall Winterspring.

WIDE SHOT:

Suddenly Buffalo Bob chooses just me
to come on stage and take his and Clarabell the Clown's
hands and jump over a low, white picket fence around

a fake turquoise pool. I am special and everything will be
all right now. Clarabell the Clown was mute for the entire
six-year run of the show until the last episode
when she said, "Goodbye kids."

The faces of Lego people are growing angrier

as they mimic their Maker. Must be an Old
Testament toy factory. With young Chinese women
in airless rooms
with just a touch of lightning when the power cuts.
Long hours with no air create a tribe. A tribe
whose fingers do repetitive tasks. Repetitive
tasks.

Masks make faces
afterthoughts.

DISSOLVE TO:

Numerous suicide nets hung
between buildings like laundry.

FOOT IN THE DOOR

Oedipus, *Oidípous* meaning 'swollen foot'

. . . and everything seems Greek tragedy now:

meet my father at the crossroads, hex on my DNA

doorway, an evermore-expanse, earth-embittered and I

move by telekinesis into the clean/dirty, sugar babies cry

in their cages, addicts come home to their shadows like late

trees, everyone holds phones in their hands like bars of soap,

and these time-storms crash invisibly like two entangled

particles separated, waving goodbye see you later! . . my mother's

Benedictine-colored hair like a slow-burning candle in the car light

as my father ushers her into the rented bungalow, the grass singing

gimlet green because give the man and woman *something* to meld

them close like Fort Knox honey as they come in from the salt wind

of Provincetown just married, scratched, strewn across that sandy floor, he/her, she/him, cross sex reflections as streams run down

their hips together like . . . together like a metronome that keeps music

even, better, shiny arrow not stopping whether or not you scream

now or later, whether you murder or just let a little blood, because I

was nothing (and am still a distillation of nothing) in their prophecies,

the twisted blind man's stick, and still, breach, I was born.

THE LAST TIME I SAW RAINER MARIA RILKE

You go back there when you can.
To the field struck bright as if born from fire.
The restive trees, grass, sky, still and cool
as a finished puzzle.
The secret self not yet ravaged.

This is where you find him.
But mostly, you have lived like an eternal expatriate
from the country of belonging.
To put aside one's own name like a broken toy.

There's a vertigo that passes for illumination—
electromagnetic addiction.
He never knew this.
The bridle that keeps you from straying
all the way to the errancy, flight, and the coming on of clouds,
the clear air that should be your birthright.

But after you lift your fingers from the most unmusical
of keys, you know you need him more than ever.

You go back there as soon as you can.
To the field where the rain ticks on the lucent grass
like the strings' pizzicato.
Part of you wanting to stay.
Part of you called back to this reckless world.

Remember the true earth with its messages you read
through the soles of your feet when spring burgeoned there?
And now things conspire to tell us nothing, half
in shame, half in unspoken hope.
That we still might rescue them,
like the violin he heard from a window
giving itself to someone.

ACKNOWLEDGMENTS

Grateful acknowledgment to the editors of the following publications in which these poems first appeared, sometimes in different versions.

Barrow Street: "The Last Time I Saw Kurt Schwitters," "The Last Time I Saw Janis Joplin"

Enchanting Verses: "Incompleteness Theory"

Gettysburg Review: "The Last Time I Saw Paul Cézanne," "The Last Time I Saw Rainer Maria Rilke"

The Huffington Post: "The Last Time I Saw Virginia Woolf," "Bickering in the Bathroom Mirror," and "On the Occasion of the Nautilus Shell"

The poem "The Last Time I Saw Virginia Woolf" was chosen by Suzanne Slavick, Chair of the Carnegie-Mellon Arts Department as the only poem to be included in an anti-gun visual art show called "Unloaded," which is touring the U.S. for three years from 2016-2019.

The Journal: "She Recounts the Amnesia of the Future"

LE Poetry: "Vultures, When They Eat They're Called A Wake," "The Moths," "Body Politics," "Diorama," "Jewish Party," "From An Imprint," and "The Last Time I Heard Thelonius Sphere Monk"

Pool: "Half the Landscape," "The Last Time I Saw Antonin Artaud," "The Last Time I Saw Delphine Seyrig," "The Last Time I Saw Samuel Beckett," and "Dream House"

Ploughshares: "You, Back from Exile"

Poet's Corner: Fieralingua (Italy) trans. Marilu' Ricci, "You, Back From Exile"

Prairie Schooner: "Dear Water" (in part)

Terminus Magazine: "Leda, Outside Bisbee, Arizona" and "Foot in the Door"

NOTES

The Last Time I Saw Paul Cézanne, page 3
He made many paintings of L'Estaque, a town near his home in
Aix-en-Provence, France.

Bickering in the Bathroom Mirror, page 8
Anteros is the god of requited love.

You, Back From Exile, page 10
This poem owes some of its lines to Frederick Sommer's "The Poetic Logic of
Art and Aesthetics," 1972. The poem refers to actor Carole Lombard's death in
an airplane crash at the age of 33.

Incompleteness Theory, page 11
This title refers to the German mathematician Kurt Gödel's Incompleteness
Theorem.

Leda, Outside Bisbee, Arizona, page 13
Leda and the Swan is a story and subject for art from Greek mythology where
Zeus turns himself into a swan and rapes Leda.

The Last Time I Saw Samuel Beckett, page 16
The italicized lines are Beckett's.

Time Crunch, page 21
The italicized lines are from Gerard Manley Hopkins, Theodore Roethke,
Virginia Woolf and Paul Celan.

The Last Time I Saw Virginia Woolf, page 25
Woolf suffered a life-long chemical imbalance that caused her to have periods
of what her family termed "madness." She most probably suffered from
bipolar disorder. Most of her life was happy and productive. Her suicide in
the River Ouse near her country house, Monk's House, Rodmell, England was
concomitant with the bombing over and around that house, where she resided
during World War II.

The Last Time I Saw Antonin Artaud, page 32

Artaud was a French playwright, poet, theater director and actor who played the part of Jean-Paul Marat in Abel Gance's film *Napoleon*. A prolific and highly original artist, Artaud often shocked audiences with his unusual gestures and sounds. He also suffered from bouts of schizophrenia that increased as he aged.

The Last Time I Saw Kurt Schwitters, page 37

Schwitters was a German painter who worked in several genres and movements including Dadaism, Constructivism, Surrealism, poetry, sculpture and what came to be known as installation art.

He is most famous for his collages, which he called *Merz pictures*. During World War I he felt that everything became fragmented around him and that "new things had to be made out of the fragments" of the past and that was *Merz*. His work was included in a Nazi exhibition of "degenerate art" and he had to flee Germany during World War II.

While Deuterium and Tritium Spread, page 44

Deuterium and Tritium are hydrogen isotopes dangerous to living matter. Fukushima is still cleaning up the Tritium that was released when the tsunami damaged the Fukushima Nuclear Power Plant after the March 11, 2011, earthquake in Japan.

She Recounts the Amnesia of the Future, page 46

This poem references Ezra Pound's use of Ernest Fenallosa's essays on the Chinese ideogram as an early way of making images through written language. Pound's founding of Imagism owed much to his fervent reading of Fenallosa's study. When Pound was institutionalized, he complained repeatedly of "not being able to lie flat enough."

Thomas Bernhard, Austrian author of *Concrete, Wittgenstein's Nephew* and many other books, is one of my favorite novelists. The protagonists in many of his books sustain hilarious, profound and complex *complaints* that are both peculiarly Bernhard and deeply universal.

The Last Time I Saw Delphine Seyrig, page 53

Seyrig was a French stage and film actor, director, and feminist who starred in such films as Alain Resnais' *Last Year At Marienbad* and Chantal Akerman's *Jeanne Diehlman, 23 quai du Commerce, 1080 Bruxelles.*

Everything Must Go, page 62
The italicized lines are actual facts gleaned from various sources. Note: I wrote the first part of this poem quite a few years before Texas became a purple, or possibly, eventually a blue, state. Either way, I apologize.

The Last Time I Saw Rainer Maria Rilke, page 69
The italicized lines are Rilke's.

CATHY COLMAN'S first book, *Borrowed Dress*, won the 2001 Felix Pollak Prize for Poetry and was on the *The Los Angeles Times* Bestseller List the first week of its release. Her second collection, *Beauty's Tattoo*, was published by Tebot Bach Publications. Her poetry has appeared in *The Gettysburg Review, The Huffington Post, The Colorado Review, Ploughshares, Prairie Schooner, The Journal, Barrow Street, The Southern Review, The Los Angeles Review, Quarterly West, Pool, Chance of a Ghost Anthology (Putnam/Tarcher), Writers on Writing (Putnam)*, and elsewhere. She has won the Browning Award for Poetry and the Ascher Montandon Award for Poetry. She has been nominated for a Pushcart Prize seven times and was a former reviewer for *The New York Times Book Review*. Her work has been translated into Italian, Croatian and Russian.

WHAT BOOKS PRESS

LOS ANGELES